God's Will

Inviting & Exciting

By: Valerie Anne Todd Listman

Dedication

As I write this book from a prison cell in a state correctional institute, I want to give God my highest praise. I am absolutely nothing with out Jesus Christ!

I have been abandoned, abused, homeless, drug-addicted, pitiful and pathetic.

I dedicate this book to my Lord and savior who visits me everyday in a prison cell and cares about every single detail of my life. I have a amazing oneness with Jesus that can not be severed. He is the reason I live, move, and have my being.

I also dedicate this book to my husband Timothy Leonard Listman. He is my Jesus on earth. I also like to dedicate this book to my precious four children and my step daughter. John Michael Green Jr, is a pillar of strength, and thoughtfulness. Desiree Alyce Hunsberger is my angel on earth. Tor Joseph McGregor Jr. is a friend of God, and pure delight. Ian Tor McGregor is my miracle child and so carefree.

Last but not least, is my step daughter Heaven Lee Listman who is intelligent and tender hearted.

Table of Contents

Day 11: Do not be afraid remember the Lord (Nehemiah 4:14)

Day 12: You are the Father! God can not forsake His own

Day 13: Because you said it, I will do it.

Day 14: Give life flavor, be the salt of the earth.

Day 15: Deliverance

Day 16: Expectation

Day 17: Wait well

Day 18: God has a plan, walk in His will

Day 19: Sacrificial living is a privilege

Day 20: It is not God's will for you to be carrying heavy burdens, His burden is light

Day 21: By wisdom a house is built, by understanding it is established and by knowledge its chambers are filled with all precious and pleasant riches.

Day 22: If thou have thought evil lay thine hand upon thy mouth (Pr 30:32)

Introduction

I was once told that if you do something for thirty days it becomes a habit. Now I don't know about you but I've had some bad habits! So I am inviting you on an exciting thirty day adventure that will change the course of your life. You may lose yourself and find yourself. I know sometimes when we think of God's will we cringe inside, and think of the worst case scenario however, God is outside of time and space and what He has in store for you is beyond your wildest dreams. God is love! He is the maker of love and an inexhaustible source of love. Therefore, why not make a new habit to bask in God's love, and will for the next thirty days?

"God has a plan for your pain"

For the short time that we live on this earth
Let's embrace our pain, and give birth
To a vision, to a purpose, to a goal, to a dream
We are not cowards, we are God's redeemed
Failure has knocked us down; we've been hit with
deaths blow,
Our hearts have been torn.
After hours of labor a baby is born.
Take your eyes off the pain, it will not destroy
Weeping endures for the night, and then comes the joy
Flowers will not grow with any rain.
Pick up your mat, God has a plan for your pain.

Day One

"In everything give thanks for this is the will of God in Christ Jesus concerning you" 1Thes 5:18

In everything give thanks, even during an awful experience. You've got to be kidding me! Is this some kind of sick joke? No, this isn't a joke at all. This is serious business. Get on your knees and thank God; remain standing and thank God; thank Him while you're driving, swimming, skating, fishing, crying, running, walking and talking. First of all we need to thank Him because He deserves to be thanked!

I'm quite sure it wasn't any human being who made the sun rise this morning, and gave every living soul their breath. I live, move and breathe because of Jesus Christ.

I came into the county jail thirteen months ago with a hopeless state of mind. I was scattered all over the place with racing thoughts, emotionally distraught, and beaten down physically. I thought I was beyond repair and redemption. Jesus stooped down into a jail cell and tenderly nurtured me emotionally, mentally, and physically. He did a quick work on me, and all I could think about doing all day, every day is continually thank Him.

Joy unspeakable comes upon me like a rushing wind and lifts me higher and higher with each passing day that I kneel in His presence to thank Him

The measure of love I receive by the minute can not be weighed on a human scale, after all how can we measure the measureless? Jesus keeps me satisfied, wanting nothing more but more of Him.

When God explodes in your life like dynamite , you can't do anything but thank Him.

It hurts to be away from my children, husband, and loved ones. However, God didn't put me here. As a matter of fact God blessed my mess. I am so grateful to have a forgiving Father, a listening friend available at all times, that it humbles me.

When I think about how small my part in this universe is, and yet I am significant to the Almighty God. I can't help but to be thankful.

Did you ever go out of your way for someone? Or give someone a gift and they never said thank you or even acknowledged you? It's pretty painful, isn't it. I wonder of God feels. He gave us a gift that lasts beyond this life time… His one and only Son Jesus. If God didn't do another thing for me, He did enough already by giving His Son to die in my place. Yet God doesn't stop there. Jesus came to give us life and to give it more abundantly. John 10:10

I was curious about this abundant life, so I started digging into the bible to find the hidden treasures that were missing from my life. I realized I have been living under my privileges and that I was born for more than this. There isn't a single person in this entire world that could convince me that the bible isn't alive and active and sharper than any two edged sword.

I have lost myself and found myself through God's written word. Jesus is the realest person in my life and He is invisible.

When they stripped searched me, I thank God, when I use the bathroom in front of my cell mate I thank God, when I don't get mail I thank God, and when they call us for meals I thank God. My point is this, if I can thank God, so can you!

Start thanking God and watch what a difference it makes. If God has the very best in store for you, and it is His will for you to give thanks, start giving thanks and the best is yet to come.

"Nothing hits harder than life"

Nothing hits harder than life
not a man, not a gun
When there is nowhere to run
not a double-edged knife.
When I was a baby
No one stopped to think maybe
I was worth the breath that he gave me
My mom was a prostitute, my dad was a fag
I don't care about style, I don't care about swag
I'm working these steps I'm in my bag
Step 1 I can't step 2 He can
Step 3 I'll let Him unfold his plan
I'll be fearless and thorough and get rid of this dirt
If I keep it inside I'm the one who get's hurt
These defects are killing me, now and in the past
Get rid of these short comings I humbly ask
I won't stop till I get it. Get it!
And when I'm wrong I'll promptly admit it
This is my life I can't hesitate
I'll talk to Jesus, listen and meditate
This last step is selfless it's not about me
I will help others in their recovery
A prevention plan I must prepare
That's all I got thank you all for letting me share

Day Two

"I say, "your will be done" yet, I expect God to submit to my will."

I am a funny character. I'm sure I make God fall off His throne laughing at me. Some of my bold request I had made Him smile I'm sure. I know He answers yes, no, wait, and you got to be kidding me Valerie!!! I say, Jesus you said ask and I will receive now stick to your word. Then I go to His throne of grace boldly as if I will not take no for an answer.

I have used every avenue to convince God that my will was better then His. Don't misunderstand me, I do ask and receive, I do seek and find, I do knock and the door comes flying open. I do go to His throne of grace boldly with full assurance that He inclines His Holy ears to me.

I'm talking about times I have tried to control and manipulate and persuade God into thinking what I was asking for was good for me. I learn that God's ways are so much higher than mine. I have also learn to appreciate His infinite wisdom as I look back and see why He said no! As I continue to study His word and abide in Him, and allow Him to make himself at home inside of me , I start wanting what he wants because it is real and lasting.

I have done things my way for years and it has been pointless and meaningless. I have jump in and out of relationships, purchased brand new cars, lived in beautiful homes, tried every drug you can image, went from employment to employment searching for anything real and lasting and came up empty.

My will has usually been self-centered, self-absorbed, for my own self-satisfaction. However, the closer I get to Jesus has made realize how different him and I are. You see as I read the gospel of Jesus Christ I can clearly see that it was about his Fathers will and others, and look where it landedHim; seated at the right side of his Father. Jesus summed it up for us when he said, "love the Lord your God with all your heart, soul, strength, and mind, and love your neighbor as yourself." Now that has become my will.

Everyday I set out to love God through kind and loving acts to others. His will is so fulfilling. I actually gain a better perspective in my own life by loving and helping others. Today why don't you join me in the will of God and make it your aim to love everyone you come in contact with. It can be as simple as giving someone a smile that doesn't have one. God's will not mine.

"Jesus said"

Jesus said, "In this world you will have tribulation"
With it's ups and downs, twist and turns
Lessons learned
With it's ins and outs
Fears and doubts
Jesus said, "Be of good cheer I have overcome this
world"
He's inside of me
Beside me
Guiding me
He's bigger, stronger, greater than the enemy
that's riding me
Jesus said, "You are the light of the world and the salt
of the earth
He knit me together and smiled at my birth
He's the one who determines my worth
Jesus said, "Do not be afraid I am with you"
Let every man be a liar and God be true
Is anything too hard for the Lord to do?
He never broke a promise since He came into
my heart
When I get to my red sea the waters will part
He's all I'm living for
He's the same yesterday, today, and forevermore

Day Three

"Living under your privileges"

There is a story in the new testament in the gospel according to Luke chapter 15:11-32 about a prodigal son who squanders everything he has in reckless living. I can definitely relate big time with this son. I have lived recklessly and irresponsible. I accepted a lot of stuff that I should have rejected. Verbal and physical abuse I accepted as normal.

As I take a good, hard look at my life right now I realize I lived under my privileges. Which brings me to the second son, in Luke chapter fifteen. You see when the other son came to his senses, after losing everything and went back to his father, his father had a celebration with a feast, and the other brother was hurt , angry, and bitter.

When he went to his father he said, "All these years I have worked for you and obeyed your orders and what have you given me? Not even a goat to have a feast with my friends." Yet the father answered, "You are always here with me and everything I have is yours."

Wow!!! All those years he could have been having a feast and celebration every single day, but he was living under his privileges.

When Jesus said, "The thief comes to steal, kill, and destroy, but I come so that you may have life and have life more abundantly." (John 10:10) He wasn't playing.

We are not serving some poor fellow from Galilee. We are serving a Lord that has a power in him that death and the grave couldn't hold down.

When I accepted Jesus Christ into my heart, all that is His is now mine. That's the too-good-to-be-true news of the Gospel. It is why I wake up with joy like a perpetual fountain in my soul. It is why I lay my head on my pillow and rest safely and securely. It is why I feel cherished and adored every second of the day. It is why my circumstances will never negate my royal position seated with Christ.

This is a truth that's needs to be unleashed in your soul; everything I have is yours! Since God owns it all, we definitely have financial security as well as emotional security, and physical security. Jesus is the same yesterday, today, and forever. By His stripes we are healed. God will supply all our needs according to His riches. His riches are inexhaustible.

I don't have people anxious to send me money, however, I have never lacked one good thing since I have been in prison. As a matter of fact, I'm an exercise person so I walk two hours a day and I had a hole in the bottom of my sneakers and only Jesus and I knew about it. So I got on my knees and I said, "Lord, please go into someone's heart to help me financially" I left it up to God what He was going to do. I didn't know how he was going to do it.

One day, a woman I hardly knew came to my cell door and said that God told her to buy me sneakers, and needless to say I started crying in gratitude and wonder.

This is only one incident however there has been one after another. God will not forsake His own, and every good and perfect gift is from the Father of lights. I refuse to live under my privileges any longer. What God has for me is above everything I have thought or dreamed of. Why don't you find out what God has in store for you and stop living under your privileges

"100%"

What can I give you? You have all these galaxies, countries and lands.

I'll give to the poor, I'll hug somebody, I'll give you my hands.

What can I give you? You have the sharks, the lions, the birds.

I'll encourage some today, I'll bless someone, I'll give You my words

What can I give you? You have the ocean, the sky, the trees.

I'll pray for someone today, I'll give you my knees.

What can I give you? You have everything, each and every part.

I'll love someone today, I'll give you my heart.

What can I give you? Your only Son you have sent.

I'll give you all of me, I'll give you 100%

Day Four

"Healthy until it is unhealthy"

Today I am talking about extreme behavior and thought patterns. I am writing in regards to things that are healthy until they start to consume you. God has not given me a sound mind to store useless information, yet I have taken the healthiest thing and made it unhealthy.

God always has to redirect my way of thinking. For example, I exercise on a daily basis. Now that doesn't sound unhealthy at all does it? Well, it is when you take it to the extreme that I do. I set goals for myself everyday and when I don't reach my set goal, I can't relax and it consumes me. That is where my heavenly Father breaks through my warped thinking and reminds me that the reason I exercise is to escape and relieve tension, and to keep my body fit. Why then are you turning it into something stressful? Then I yield myself to that still small voice and appreciate the time and energy I did have to exercise.

Here is another example of how I turn something healthy into something unhealthy. I set a time aside for bible reading and daily devotionals everyday. That is something very healthy and beneficial, right? Of course it is healthy until Valerie decides that she can not be interrupted by anyone or anything during this time. Then I hear a still, small, gentle whisper say, "Valerie, love your neighbor. Be kindly affectionate one to another with brotherly love because a friend loves at all times."

I am not saying spending time in scripture and exercise is wrong. I am simply saying when it becomes something it wasn't intended to be, it is unhealthy.

These two examples should show anyone just how vital it is to have a relationship with Jesus. I need Him more than my next heartbeat. When the sweet Holy Spirit abides inside of you, it is like having a navigational system tell you when you are off course.

It is God's will for me to pray, read my bible, exercise, love others and serve. How ever, God is a God of balance, restoration, renewal, and refreshment. So I must always be sensitive to the sweet whisper of the Holy Spirit as he reminds me to cease from healthy behavior that has become unhealthy.

Is there anything in your life today that seemed to be healthy, but you have taken it to the extreme and it consumes you? If there is, rid yourselves of this today by placing it into God's mighty hands and outstretched arms and allowing Him to have His way in your life. Then you can set the sails of your life to receive the wind of the Holy Spirit and be guided down a rewarding road.

"Powerful river inside me"

I must do in order to be

There is a powerful river inside of me

The river's alive and it can't be stopped

From my innermost being flow rivers of
Water that can't be topped

All the rivers flow into the sea, yet the sea
Is not full

I have a well of water perpetually flowing
According to God's will

<u>Day Five</u>

"Failure our greatest teacher"

Let's face it; failure is a part of life. Now lets really face failure as the courageous men and woman that God created us to be. Failure is going to be one of two things: a stumbling block or a stepping stone. Our attitude about failure can be one of despair or one of discovery and growth.

I can write four books on my failures alone. However, I choose to view my failures as my greatest teacher. Even the apostle Paul said, "I have learned, I have learned, I have learned." there is no end to learning. Great men and woman have failed over and over again. What has made them great men and woman is learning from their failures and starting over.

Today is the day to acknowledge your failures look at them square in the face and allow them to teach you about yourself and recognize what has not worked for you. Drugs, relationships, food, shopping, gambling, complicating everything, pride, fear, guilt, disobedience, being judgmental, procrastination, laziness, worry, lying, and manipulation; these are just a few of the ways I have failed. These are shortcuts I have taken that have ended up being the long road.

You may wonder what failure has to do with God's will being exciting and inviting. Failure has nothing to do with God's will because God cannot fail! The inviting and exciting part is what God is able to do with our failures. Obstacles mean nothing to God. Strongholds and failures will mean nothing to me. I will keep striving to reach what is ahead. Life is full of tests. Jesus is the answer to every test. Now that I have given you the answer to the test, failing should be very hard for you to do!

"Victims awareness class"

This class has forced me to take a good hard look at myself, and redirect my time.

I have seen the pain I've cause the community, my children, my spouse, and the victims of my crime.

I question my humanity with the choices I select.

One drink, one drug, one bad decision has a rippling effect.

It hurts my heart to hear the number of the death statistics,

It really hits home with the pain I've inflicted.

Failure can be your greatest teacher if your willing to learn.

I have a pulse, I have a purpose, I made the right turn.

This was an eye opening experience that left me with a tremendous amount of gratitude.

My thoughts and feelings have changed,

I have a brand new attitude.

Day Six

"Struggle well"

Anyone who doesn't think that there will be struggles in this life on earth is highly mistaken! Today I am presenting a challenge to you, which is, when you do struggle, struggle well! This is what the apostle Paul is talking about when he says that believers are more than conquerors through Christ who loves us (Romans 8:37).

During my times of struggling and struggling well, I have come out of the battle with more than what I came in with, that is more than a conqueror! Before I tell you about struggling well, I am going to tell you about the crutches I've used when I didn't struggle well.

One of the things I use to do when I struggled was sleep. I didn't want to face the day, I didn't want to be bothered by anyone, and I certainly didn't want to think, feel, or deal with anything. Therefore, I figured I would just sleep it away. I told you I am a funny character.

The bible says, " Love not sleep lest you come to poverty" (Proverbs 20:13). How am I going to be responsible, reliable, dependable, and productive while I am sleeping?

Another crutch I used was drugs and alcohol. This way the numbing effect, so I thought, needless to say this only magnified my problems. Then of course, I used relationships as a crutch. This was my way of switching the focus off of myself and shifting it on to another person. However, it is impossible for any one person to make another person feel full.

I also used food as a crutch and hated myself when I became overweight. So now that we have looked at useless ways of struggling, let's look at how to struggle well.

The other morning I woke up with a feeling that my heart was torn into pieces. I missed my kids and I missed my husband. I started thinking about the next thirty-two months I had ahead of me and I became distraught. The first thing I did was ask my Heavenly Father what His Will was for me, then I got down on my knees and began to thank and praise Him for the day that He had made and I sang to Him. I started speaking His Word over my life, circumstances, children, husband, and others. Then a breakthrough happened; I totally forgot about myself because I was concentrating on Him, and in His presence was fullness of joy just like He promised.

At that moment I realized I was not breaking down, I was breaking through into a closer walk with Jesus. When I got off my knees I wrote Jesus a letter, read the bible and my devotionals. The day that had started out unbearable had become so enjoyable. I didn't want the day to end. I came out of this struggle with way more than I went in. I had a great and glorious joy, and oasis of calmness, and I felt loved and cherished.

Had I never read the bible about people like Paul and Silas, who were thrown into prison and severely beaten and still prayed and sang hymns to Jesus, I would not have known how to deal with my struggles.

Today if you are struggling look away from yourself and look unto Jesus. He will turn your day upside down, inside out, and unbelievably joyful. Trade your struggle in for His joy unspeakable. God is faithful. He can not lie, so hold on to His Unchanging Hand and struggle well

"Before the sunrise"

As I awaken to a brand new day,
I greet it with a smile.

I humbly get on my knees
And I stay there for awhile

I thank Him that I am able to see, hear,
Smell, breathe, and talk,

I ask Him to order my steps
Wherever I may walk

I need this vital union
With my Father, Lord, and Friend

I praise Him and bless His name
And I wish this time would never end.

I realize why Jesus awoke before the day
And found a solitary place

There's no greater privilege
Than to seek the glory of the Lord's Face.

I catch a glimpse of my Creator
Right before my eyes,

When I pray, praise, and abide
Before the sunrise.

Day Seven

"You can't lose when you are a winner"

God is great! Is anything too hard for the Lord? Well let's look at a couple impossibilities, and answer that question for ourselves. Can a virgin get pregnant? Can donkey's speak? Can water part all by itself and become dry land?

My point is this; there is a God in Heaven who specializes in impossibilities!! He is able to do anything! However, the really great thing about God is that although He is high, mighty, powerful and perfect, He is willing to make His home inside of anyone who invites Him into their heart.

I can tell you first hand because I invited Him into my heart. He has exploded like dynamite inside of me!

According to this world, I look like a loser, Yet I have the Creator of Heaven and earth living inside of me and that makes me a winner!

God says that those who set their heart on me, I will show my power on their behalf (IChronicles16:9). I can't lose!! I am more than a conqueror. I can do all things through Christ who strengthens me! I take God at His word that will never pass away, and He has done incredible, outstanding, unreal things right before my eyes.

Despite the fact that I have been a junkie, a liar, a thief, an adulteress, and much more, God says that I am accepted!! This is very good super duper news!! As a matter of fact it is too good to be true.

The one who is able to destroy both body and soul accepts me. On top of this awesome acceptance God seals me with the Holy-Spirit of promise!

I can not lose! Failure is alien to God's nature, I am what He says I am. Today is the day to agree with God and believe what He says you are. You are a winner!!

" To my husband, friend and brother
Tim Listman "

"What he treasures most"

I can tell what you value
By your words and what you buy,

When this world no longer matters
And selfishness begins to die,

When the first thing you purchase
Is God's living word,

There's not a shadow of doubt
That your spirit has been stirred.

Jesus is consistently constant
So hold on to his unchanging hands

Our marriage covenant is so vital to you,
That's why you bought those wedding bands.

For where your treasure is,
Your heart will always be,

Tim, your heart is not bound to this world,
Your heart is heavenly

God is on your side
And the whole heavenly host

When you bought that bible and provided for your
wife,
You showed what you treasure most.

Day Eight

*"Cast your cares on Jesus, and then you
won't have a care in this world"*

I have an oasis of calmness. I literally do not have a care
in this world; I make a choice every day to cast my
cares on Jesus. It is a divine shift, taken off of my
shoulders and placed onto Jesus, who is able to do
exceedingly, immeasurably, abundantly above
anything that I can do.

When I take things into my own hands things can get
pretty ugly. I can be impulsive, anxious, destructive,
and dangerous. So why in the world would I handle
anything when I can give it to Jesus, who walked this
earth and was tempted in every way yet, without sin!?
This seems to be a no-brainer, Jesus said, "Come unto
me all ye that labor and are heavy laden and I will give
you rest." (Matt11:28) Peter, a disciple of Jesus said,
"Casting all your care upon Him for he careth for you."
(1Pet 5:7)

If there were a ton of cinder blocks on top of you, and there was a weight lifter who was willing to remove them from you, wouldn't you let him? Jesus is willing to take your burdens and make your load light. Whatever is weighing you down today give it to Jesus.

You may wonder just how to give it to Jesus and be carefree, so I will tell you how I do it. Yesterday morning they called my name and told me to put on all my state clothing because I was going to an outside hospital trip. Well, being as though I am in excellent health this came as a surprise so I immediately got on my knees and said to God, "you are the great physician and by Jesus stripes I am healed, and I do not believe the report of man I believe in your Holy word and you said if thou canst believe, all things are possible to him that believeth and I am asking you to go before me and work all things for my good because I definitely love you and I am called according to your purpose and you can not forsake your own so please take this ride to the hospital with me and spend this entire day with me in Jesus name amen."

After I got done praying I felt very light almost as if I was floating, and I knew beyond a shadow of a doubt that God was with me therefore no one could be against me.

They shackled me, handcuffed me, and placed me into a correction van. I watched the guards load their guns before leaving the state grounds. However, I didn't have a care in this world. I looked at the majestic mountains, I saw leaves falling from trees, and I looked at many houses that were decorated for Halloween. When we arrived at the hospital I seen a doctor who asked me if I had numerous symptoms of a hyper thyroid that they found in my blood work. I did not have even one symptom so they will do a follow up in the next couple months.

I enjoyed the ride back to the prison and I enjoyed my God the whole time. I did not get all frantic and start thinking the worst I believe the bible in it's entirety and it proves itself true every time. I make a quality decision every day and refuse to take my cares upon myself. I cast my cares upon Jesus and then I don't have a care in this world.

To my son Johnny, who is my twin and a pillar of unending strength
"Johnny you are a winner"

Since the day that you were born, you were always my
Little guy

Your smile, your laugh, your personality puts a sparkle
in my eye.
You have extraordinary qualities and you're unique in
Every way
You're constantly on my mind, and in my prayers each
and every day
I know life has been hard, and you experienced a lot of
Pain.

We'd never see a rainbow if there wasn't any rain!

You are no longer a child, into a man you've grown
You're about to be a father and have a baby of your
own
Don't worry what your up against, just be who you

Always been

You can't lose Johnny, that's why you always
win!!!!!!!!!!

Day Nine

"Enjoying relationships instead of destroying them"

Life is full of relationships. Whether it is your spouse, your child, your parents, your co-worker, your friends, your sister, or your brother, it is inevitable that we should learn to make the most of relationships.

Now, I am no expert on relationships, as a matter of fact I have built walls higher than Jericho so that no one could get to know me. I have been disloyal, dishonest, and very disturbing. I grew up in a family where no one trusted each other, no one respected each other, and no one valued each other. Therefore, love was absent.

As a result of this I came into every relationship with my preconceptions of the other person. I always thought people had hidden selfish agenda's and I wondered what they were up to. I always thought people were lying, insincere, and untrustworthy. My thinking has been absolutely wrong for thirty six years concerning relationships. I have been using a faulty mental map. Do you know what will happen, if the map you are using is incorrect? You will never get to your destination.

One afternoon I was lying on my bunk in my cell and the Sweet Holy Spirit said, "Valerie why don't you start enjoying relationships, and looking at people as the irreplaceable treasures that they are?!"

It was like scales were removed from my eyes and I started viewing relationships much different. I see the very best in people and I don't criticize anyone. All those years of being skeptical of everyone I met was not God's will. The enemy of my soul is the one who sows the seeds of suspicion and accusation. In other words, I was doing the devil's dirty work, anytime I destroyed relationships. After all isn't that what he comes to do, steal, kill, and destroy.

Think about it, how many relationships may have prospered and been fruitful if you hadn't been so suspicious? I mean I am not jumping to conclusions any longer especially when I have absolutely no facts. It is certainly God's will that I love my neighbor. Love is a decision!! So how about making a decision today to see the very best in everyone and start enjoying relationships instead of destroying them.

**To my one and only daughter
Desiree Alyce,
She is my visible angel.**

"My Treasure"

On rainy days you are my sunshine in this world.

You're growing up but your still my little girl.

This is not an end; this is a brand new start.

Desiree, if you want to see your reflection just look
inside my heart.

The love I have for you is beyond measure,

When God created you He gave me a treasure.

Day Ten

*"It is God's will for you to smile.
Rejoice is not a suggestion."*

Rejoice in the Lord always, and again I say rejoice
(Philippians 4:4)

Wow! You mean I don't have to take everything so
serious, God wants me to rejoice? Do you mean that
God's business is so serious that we can't smile? This is
the day that the Lord has made I will rejoice and be
glad in it!!!! (Psalms 118:24).

People who walked closely to our Lord knew the
importance of rejoicing. Why else would Paul say it
twice in one sentence? I make a prayerful choice
everyday to rejoice. I don't know about you but I
would much rather laugh, smile, and be cheerful than
to cry, frown, and be somber. The reason I smile is
because I know God is smiling down on me!

When I wake up I imagine the smile of God and immediately I smile. Did you ever watch your child sleep? Doesn't that make you smile? Did you ever watch your child play with action figures or dolls? Does that make you smile? Did you ever hear your child sing? Doesn't that make you smile? Well, I believe that God is way greater than any human being, so if I smile at my child I am quite sure that God is smiling down on His children. After all we are made in His image. You'll never get to know the smile of God if you never get to know God however, if you get to know God you will never stop smiling. I am smiling from ear to ear in a small prison cell as I write this today so surely you can smile and rejoice no matter what life throws at us.

We are not puppets being strung along by the whims and moods of others or the weather outside, our joy will never come from the outer-circumstance. We are God's chosen generation, a royal priesthood called out of darkness into His marvelous light.

I can't help but to rejoice, I am not a slave to this fallen world no more, I am free to be me, and I walk in the liberty of God's great love everyday and that is enough to make me smile. Rejoice is not a suggestion it is a command. Do God's will today and smile.

To my second son
Tor
The very friendly one

"Tor"

Throughout my whole pregnancy I smiled, and was full of joy.

I knew inside my belly was an awesome little boy!!

When God gave me you He gave me everything.

I love the way you play, and I love the way you sing.

From the first time I laid eyes on you, I knew you were all I could ask for.

You have always made me smile, and you always will Tor!!!

Day Eleven

"Do not be afraid, remember the Lord"

There was a time I lived in constant fear, I was afraid to take risks. I was afraid to be myself because I thought that no one would like, or accept me. I was afraid of sudden danger, I thought of the worst possible scenario, and I believed it was going to happen to me. This is an awful way to live. I do not live in fear any longer!! However, this did not happen all at once for me, it was a gradual process.

I would read the bible and God would tell me things like, "Look at the birds, up there in the sky, I feed them Valerie, don't you think I will feed you?" and He would tell me," why are you walking around with these heavy burdens when I will make your load light?" and over and over and over He would tell me "Do not be afraid I am with you and if I am with you who could possibly be against you."

So I started taking God at His word. I started believing that He would take care of me and make my load light. I started believing that He was with me every step of the way. I started believing that I didn't have a spirit of fear. I started believing the Truth and fear withered away. I started seeing what I believed. It is so amazing to see results and outcomes just the way He said it would be.

Now, I have something to remember when fear tries to slip back into my life. I remember the Lord, and His faithfulness and I feed off of His faithfulness. However, if you never take God at His word and build memories with Him you can never remember the Lord.

Do not be afraid to dive in to see the miraculous happen. God has not given you a spirit of fear He has given you a spirit of power, love and a sound mind.

When fear enters you mind it is definitely not from God because what ever comes your way I am quite sure God can handle it without being damaged one bit. Do not be afraid today, remember the Lord.

**To my last son
Ian
Who is my miracle baby**

"Ian... My miracle boy!"

Tender, gentle and peaceful is what you are.

When I look into the sky you are my shining star.

You are my only child with precious brown eyes.

Everything about you is one big surprise!!

You are very good at whatever you do,

The reason your middle name is Tor is because your
dad wanted to name

You after him too.

You make me happy and my heart so full of joy!

Ian you are my miracle boy!!!

Day Twelve

"You are the father!!! God can not forsake His own."

Have you watched the Maury show? Most of his episodes are about paternity tests, trying to prove who the father of that child is. If that fathers blood is flowing through the child, Maury proclaims, "You are the father!" then the audience goes crazy applauding because the child is no longer fatherless.

My biological father has never laid his eyes on me, I did however, grow up with a daddy who pistol-whipped my mom(grand-mom), molested me, shot my sister, and hung his self by the time I was ten years old. Needless to say, I wasn't to fond of father figures or men in general. Yet, inside me there was a hunger, a longing to be loved, accepted, and identified as someone special and valuable. I tried to fill this hunger with everything this world offered, and my heart was still leaking.

In 1994 I gladly received Jesus into my heart to be my savior and friend and boy is He. However, I wasn't willing to get close to a father. I did my talking to Jesus and the Sweet Holy-Spirit.

In 2009 I finally opened my heart and my arms to my Heavenly Father. He has remained faithful, consistent, loving, gracious, merciful, and kind all these years that I resisted His everlasting love. He has never forced His way in my life. He has won me over with His nurturing nature.

I love the way He loves me, I feel so cherished, I feel so valued. He said, " Valerie, you are accepted in the beloved, and you are gloriously complete" I hear Him telling me, "It is my good pleasure to give you the kingdom." He treats me like a princess.

I didn't realize that in 1994 when I received Jesus that his blood was flowing through me and I can now proclaim to God, " You are the Father!!" I am not fatherless, and the good thing about God is that He can not forsake His own. He is with me always protecting me and shielding me with favor and love.

If you feel fatherless today it is not God's fault and it is not true. You have a Father in Heaven that wants you to jump on His lap, and wrap your arms around His neck and never let go. Are you willing to let go of all your false notions about your Heavenly Father, and embrace Him today and ever more? Don't let another day pass without the Father's Love.

"To my precious
one and only step-daughter
Heaven Lee"

"Heaven Lee"

A child locked inside her world of pain,

Sometimes on sunny days she still feel the rain.

She's a writer, she's a singer and so sweet in her own
special way.

She's afraid to let anyone get close to her because of the
price her heart will pay.

Jesus leap inside of her and set her heart free.

She's my one and only step-daughter and her name is
Heaven Lee!!

Day Thirteen

"Because you said it, I will do it"

Obedience is definitely God's Will!!! The awesome part about obeying God is the outcome. There is a story in Luke chapter 5 verses 3-5, apparently Peter had toiled all night fishing Yet, He caught nothing. Jesus tells Peter to let his net down to catch some fish. Peter explains to Jesus that he had been fishing all night and He caught nothing, never the less, at thy Word I will let down the net. In other words, because you said it I will do it.

What happens next really blows me away: Peter's net was so full of fish that it began to break and he shouted to his partners that were in another boat to come help them, and they came and both the ships were filled so much that the ships began to sink!! Wow!! Obedience is very rewarding.

I am mother and I don't give my children instructions and directions because I want to control them, I give them instruction and direction because I know what is best for them.

God is older and wiser than we are, not to mention his power, majesty, and divinity. When God tells us to do something it is always for our good. Over and over again God tells me to do something and when I obey, He totally knocks me rights off of my feet with amazement, and just like Peter, I crumble and fall down at Jesus' feet in astonishment that He would use a sinner like me for His Glory.

It says in Luke 5:8, "When Simon Peter saw it, he fell down at Jesus knees saying depart from me for I am a sinful man o Lord. For he was astonished at the amount of fish they caught." I am awe struck by Jesus!!!!

I look forward to do what he says every day, and I am never disappointed. See, when Jesus is in in something we are guaranteed success. When Jesus tells you to do something, uncertainty and doubt are replaced with expectancy and wonder. It is a thrill to live in obedience to Jesus.

Can you admit with me right now that you don't know everything? Can you admit with me with right now that you are clueless of how time began, and how a sun rises? Are you willing to put your times into the Hands of the one who is timeless? The same one who told Peter to launch out into the deep to let his net down (because Jesus knows every movement of the fish). Today, I will say without question because you said it I will do it.

"On my knees I will rise"

Hopelessness, fear, despair, guilt, and shame.

It was in this bottomless pit that I called upon your name.

A living hell is what I experienced, all that was missing was fire.

Deliver my soul, make me mature enough to stop believing a lair.

I have tasted your goodness, not one thing did I lack.

I am twice yours, you made me and then you bought me back.

Surely I was born for more than this!!

I am sealed with the Holy Spirit of promise!!

When I walked according to the course of this world, I've always felt rejected.

Yet in your great mercy and love, I am
chosen and accepted.

It is one thing to get what you deserve,
your grace is one big surprise!!

Thank you for loving me, it is on my
knees I rise!!

Day Fourteen

"Give life flavor, be the salt of the earth."

Today my question to you is this; why do we have salt in a salt shaker? Potatoes would taste real bland without salt, wouldn't they? Salt is good for seasoning!!

Where ever Jesus went He seasoned that place!! Sometimes He did it with just a word. Sometimes He did it by feeding the multitudes until they were full. Sometimes He did it by letting a child jump up on His lap while he blessed that child. Sometimes he did by calming the storms in life. Jesus is our perfect example of how to be the salt of the earth.

Being the salt of the earth is God's will and God's will for each of us is perfect. God said, "I will never leave you, nor forsake you."(Hebrews 13:5). Therefore, wherever I am God is there also! So not only has He given me His perfect will in the bible, but he also lives inside me to help me to perform His perfect will accurately.

I can be the salt of the earth today by smiling at someone who doesn't have a smile. I can be the salt of the earth today by offering hope to someone who feels hopeless. I can be the salt of the earth today by listening to someone who just needs to vent. I can be the salt of the earth today by feeding a hungry person. I can be the salt of the earth today by hugging someone who feels alone.. I'm sure you heard the saying, "If you don't use it you'll lose it." that is what I call tasteless salt. What would it cost you today to hug someone, or encourage someone, or visit someone in the hospital, or bake someone cookies? These simple acts of kindness are the little difference that makes a big difference in life. If I am able to season life today your better believe and bet your bottom dollar that I will give life flavor and be the salt of the earth!!!

"Tradition of the elders"

Let's get rid of the words can't, must, and should.

God didn't give us the strength to do what only he could.

Where do we get these heavy burdens, isn't God's load light?

Why are we taking on these battles, isn't the battle His to fight?

Why are we looking at this world when we could be looking up?

The kingdom is within us, why do we wash the outside of the cup?

Where's our servants attitude to bow and wash someone's feet?

Why can't we appreciate our food and just give thanks and eat?

Let's break the tradition of the elders, and love, laugh, and live!!

The Son of man didn't come to be served but to serve and give.

Day Fifteen

"Deliverance"

Today I am going to talk about deliverance. Totally and utterly freed from bondage. This is going to get exciting if you are bound to something that consumes every drop of your time and energy. First, I want to say strongholds mean nothing to God!!!! Addiction means nothing to God!!!!! Cancer means nothing to God!!!!! Second, I am going to mention a name that is above all names, and when we call on that name all things become possible. Have you guessed it yet? YES, I'm talking about that sweet, tender, powerful name of Jesus!!!! The name of Jesus takes A.I.D.S out of your blood!! The name of Jesus will take a lunatic and give him a sound mind!

The name of Jesus restores relationships that looked beyond repair! The name of Jesus will reconcile a family that hadn't talked in years. Oh that name is like honey on my lips. I'm not blowing sunshine up your butt right now, I am telling you that nothing is too hard for God, His hands are not short! Not only is He able to deliver you, He is willing to deliver you. When the Son sets you free, you are free indeed!! God is not a man that he shall lie, and He hasn't broken a promise yet. Every time I read chapter 5 of Mark, it sends chills up and down my spine. There is a man who is possessed by an evil spirit who lived in the tombs. This is my story, I was strung out on drugs (which are an evil spirit) living with the dead, because apart from Jesus Christ there is no life. Jesus says he is the life, and he comes to give life more abundantly. Therefore, a life without Him is death, and I certainly know that to be true. Now this man that was possessed with an evil spirit saw Jesus and ran to meet Him, Jesus spoke to the spirit and commanded it to come out of the man. Only through Jesus Christ can the power of an evil spirit be overcome. I can see that evil spirit trembling. I am a living witness of the power of sin being broken, conquered, and overcome. I have left my life of sin, and I am walking in my deliverance every second of the day. I'm in love with the lover of my soul. Now after the man with the evil spirit was delivered the bible says that he was sitting there clothed, and in his right mind. Sitting means to reign look at Eph 1:6, it says, "for he has raised us from the dead along with Christ and seated us with Him in realms because we are united with Christ Jesus." deliverance isn't no joke!! Then it says he was clothed, you see, God takes our filthy rags and cloths us with a robe of righteousness. The man was also perfectly sane, in his right mind because God has not given us a spirit of fear but of love, power, and a sound mind.

Too many people get delivered and they don't maintain their deliverance. God doesn't deliver you from alcoholism for you to go sit in a bar all day and drink non-alcoholic beverages. If you don't want to slip, you stay out of slippery places!! I was bound and bent over, crippled emotionally, mentally, and spiritually. Jesus delivered me and He will do the same thing for you. He stands at the door of your heart waiting for you to open the door and let Him in, so he can free you of every thing that has you bound. Today is the day of deliverance!!!

"Reservoir"

I rested my boundaries, my limits are gone, you are outside of time.

Your voice of truth tells me that all that is yours is mine.

I picked up my mat, I took my grave clothes off, and I'm living a resurrected life!

I have access by one spirit, I been made nigh by the blood of Christ!

You made a declaration that you would never leave me, and with your Spirit I am sealed.

You have given me joy unspeakable, peace that can't be understood, and by your stripes I am healed.

You continue to lavish me with blessings, and pick me up when I fall.

Jesus Christ is the chief corner stone; He broke down the middle wall!

Every second of every day and every where I turn you are there.

I am overwhelmed with this amazing oneness that we share.

Who am I that you would adopt me and bring me up as your own?

You give me divine rest, you comfort me, I'm never alone.
You have waited, and waited, and waited on me as I wrestled with my pride.

You have never just added to my life, you have always multiplied.

I have unsearchable riches, my election is sure!

I have life more abundantly; I tapped in to the reservoir!!!

Day Sixteen

"Expectation"

"My soul, wait thou only upon God; for my expectation is from Him." (Psalms 62:5)

Did you ever hear the saying, hope for the best but expect the worst? Well this is contrary to God's will! Why in the world would I be hoping for the best and expect the worst to come my way? If my expectation is from God almighty, who works everything out for my good, and His thoughts toward me are thoughts of peace, and not of evil to give me an expected end, and his mercy and goodness are following me around, then why would I ever expect anything but goodness???

I wake up every morning with anticipation and expectation of what my lord has in store for me on this day! The reason I call him Lord is because he is so close, he is so near to me. He is so awesome in power, I really don't know what he is going to do next. He usually sweeps me off my feet by His sovereignty that is on display in the sky each and every day.

Then He shows up and shows off in a variety of ways. It can be as simple as an unexpected letter or as huge as a mountain being removed from my life. My mountain of fear has been cast out by his perfect love, my mountain of guilt is completely gone. The mountain of a 20 to 40 year sentence was cast in the sea because my God was for me and no one was against me.

I have screwed up royally with my marriage, my children, my community, and my dignity and self-respect. I have publicly shamed Jesus name, yet, God in His mercy, love, and graciousness has restored, reconciled, renewed, rebuilt, and refreshed every single relationship that I destroyed. You better believe I live in expectancy because god has given me every reason to.

The other day I received pictures of my daughter Desiree and my two younger sons Tor Jr. and Ian and my heart broke into pieces. I felt like my heart was collapsing, and The Sweet holy Spirit whispered in my ear, "embrace your pain Valerie, you will not breakdown, you will break through."

So I got on my knees and started thanking Jesus for my children and I exalted and I magnified His name, then I placed my children into His outstretched loving arms, and asked him to surround them with multitudes of angels.

Then the correctional officer came over the intercom and announced that there was a bingo game that we could go to, so I got up and told my room-mate that we have a winning spirit (The Holy Spirit) living inside of us, so let's go win some soda.

I asked the Sweet Holy Spirit, Jesus, and my Daddy to come and enjoy bingo with me and I won twice, and my room-mate won once. Even if I hadn't won I still would have enjoyed the presence of God there with me but I did win because I live in expectancy!

I expect joy unspeakable everyday! I expect peace that can not be understood everyday! I expect love that can not be measured on a human scale everyday! I have never caught God in a lie yet, so I expect the abundant life. I refuse to live disappointed and discouraged when the hope of glory lives inside of me, and hope is a very powerful force. Why don't you higher your expectancy level today, and look to the hills where your help comes from, and let your expectation come from Him!!!!!

"I am filled with real and lasting imaginations"

My real and lasting imaginations

Begin with Genesis through Revelations

From the Law of Moses to the grace dispensation.

I imagine lying on Jesus bosom as he teaches from the mount.

I imagine Him blessing little children and teaching them to count.

I imagine Him walking on water; calming all my fears.

I see Him holding close to His heart a bottle of my tears.

I imagine Him healing the man who was blind from birth.

I see Him at the well telling that woman what she's worth.

I imagine Him answering my prayers when I touch and agree.

I see Him telling Peter, "I love you, although you denied me."

My imaginations are full of love and life.

There are no more vain imaginations because I'm one with Christ!

I walk by faith, I am not moved by what I see, hear, or feel.

I am filled with imaginations that are lasting and real.

Day Seventeen

"Wait well"

But they that wait upon the Lord shall renew their strength they shall mount up with wings as eagles; they shall run, and not be weary, and they shall walk, and not faint (Isaiah 40:30)

I serve a prayer answering God!!! I've learned that one of His most valuable answers is wait. I do want to tell you that when God tells me to wait, it upsets me at first. Then I make a decision to get my emotions in check with wisdom and truth.. My first realization is that God isn't in the habit of playing mind games with me.

If God says wait it is for a very good reason, and a greater purpose. I can't see the bigger picture, but He certainly can. Now when I take all this into consideration, I make a choice to wait well. What I mean by waiting well is I still make good use of every single second, and trust God for the perfect outcome. I don't become bitter because I didn't receive the answer that I desired, just because I don't see an immediate result doesn't mean God is inactive.

Our part in this universe is so tiny, and yet sometimes we have the audacity to complain when God says wait. Thank goodness He doesn't ask for my help when he is stretching out the starry curtain of the heavens. He didn't need me when He placed the world on its foundation. I'm not the one who provides water for the fish of the sea.

When God says wait, please don't question it. He knows our strength will be renewed, He knows that when our answer comes at just the right time we will soar with wings as eagles. He knows our endurance and perseverance will rise above weariness and we will cross that finish line. He knows that during our waiting process we will walk with our heads heaven bound looking unto the author and finisher of our faith at an unstoppable pace. So yes, I will say today wait and while you are waiting, wait well!!!

"Gloriously complete"

My ways are just so bitter, and God's way's are so

sweet.

I find everything I crave for when I kneel down at His

feet.

He's hidden deep inside me quiet and discreet.

Then I bring a piece of Him to everyone I meet.

I'm nothing without Him, yet with Him I am gloriously

complete!!!

Day Eighteen

"God has a plan, walk in His will"

What is God's will, and why should I walk in it, you
may wonder. I have a few questions for you today.
Why should a child go to school? Why can't kids just
go on the highway and play ball? Why can't teenagers
buy cigarettes and beer? Why can't we have sex with
everyone who is attractive? These questions may seem
foolish, and the answer may seem obvious yet, we still
question the one with infinite wisdom for our ultimate
good. We still allow the enemy of our souls to lie to us
when he asks, "did God really say that, you will,
surely die?" yes, we do die! We die inside.

I know first hand about believing a lie, and dying. God
specifically told me not to do certain things and I did
them anyway. My peace died my self-respect withered
away, my joy was diminished, and finally there was no
hope without God!!

God's will is out of this world literally. For the same reason we would never let a child go on the highway with a ball. God instructs us through His living word to stay away from the dangers of sin. He knows the outcome, and tries to spare us of the pain.

If you really want your life to drastically change for the better, than walk in God's exciting will! God changes everything! From good to great, from ordinary to extraordinary, from failure to fabulous, from being a coward to being full of power!!!

I have settled for less and always got less than I settle for. I want more! I want more of Jesus! He said, "seek ye first the kingdom of God, and His righteousness, and all these things shall be added unto you." (Matt 6:33) His will is seeking Him first!!

Soon as you open your eyes and become alert seek Jesus, and while you are seeking Him, he is already seeking you!! This is truly time well spent. I always begin on my knees agreeing with God that I am more than a conqueror, that I can do all things through Christ who strengthens me, that this is the day that he has made and I will rejoice, (regardless of the weather or my feelings) and be glad in it.

I agree with God that there will be no temptation that can over take me because he is faithful and will provide a way of escape for me. I agree with God that I am the head and not the tail, I am above and not beneath, I am blessed coming in and will be blessed going out. Point blank: I believe God!!! I believe He is in control, I believe the sun rises on His time; I believe the waters stop where he tells them to stop. I believe He is the way, the truth and the life!!! God certainly has plans for us or else we would not be breathing. Today walk in His will of wonderful wonders!!!

"How to come boldly"

What exactly does it mean to come to your throne of grace bold?

Is it really true that you own everything, even riches untold?

Can it be that when you tell us not to worry, that your really in control?

Can I really jump on your lap, and wrap my arms around your neck?

Can I pass the inner courts, although my life has been a wreck?

Is it true that when we ask, we really will receive?

That nothing is impossible to him who will believe?

Are we really reconciled, did Jesus make everything right?

Is the battle really yours, and I no longer have to fight?

I think I'm on to something I finally see the light?

Now I get it, I can come to your throne of grace boldly

because you and I are tight!!!

Day Nineteen

"Sacrificial living is a privilege"

Today we are going to resign ourselves to God and others. A number of things take place in sacrificial living, it is the supreme way to live. It is the way Jesus lived. He labored in love always. He totally forgot about himself to love others. He gave His life!! Did it hurt ? Yes!!! Was he abandoned? Yes!! Was he rejected? Yes!! Did that stop Him? No!! it shouldn't stop us either!

The privilege of Jesus sacrifice on the cross was saving us. We are not going to burn in hell because of His sacrifice!! What a privilege. We also have access to our Heavenly Father twenty-four hours a day because of Jesus sacrifice. We also have a sweet tender Holy Spirit living inside of us because Jesus would not leave us comfortless.

Our ways are unlike God's awesome ways. Some people see sacrificing yourself or giving to others as a weakness or being taken advantage of. Yet God see's it as and honor! I feel so honored when people ask me to pray over them. I stop whatever I am doing, because tomorrow just might be too late. I make the time for others, and it is always worth it to me. I give money, time, food, drink, letters, and a listening ear because people are worth it to me.

There is no greater blessing to me than to be a blessing to someone else. Until you try it, you will never know the privilege of seeing a sparkle in someone else's eyes because you cared enough to sacrifice for them. This is the life of total loss of yourself, and a mass quantity of absolute and entire gain! It is why Jesus is seated on the right hand of God, and has been given all authority in heavens and earth, in the most privileged position, don't take my word for it, find out for yourself if sacrificial living is a privilege.

To my beloved husband
Tim
"Married Love"

On May 10th, 2008 you and I were united in Christ.

Tim, I want nothing more than to always enrich your life.

Two exotic flowers, watered often until they fully bloom,

A mental image I hold in my mind of the bride and the bride groom.

Just when we were at our wit's end, God gave us a brand new Start.

What flabbergasted me the most about you is the radiance of your heart.

The passion you possess is more than I ever dreamed of

Valentines Day can't even compare to our
Married love.

Day Twenty

"It is not God's will for you to be carrying heavy burdens, His burden is light!"

Today, I am going to point out a sure indicator of being outside of God's will, if you feel heavy, weighed down, and immobilized with burdens you are outside of God's will!!! Jesus said, "come to me all of you who are weary and carry heavy burdens and I will give you rest." (Matthew 11:28). Two verses later Jesus said, "for my yoke is easy to bear, and the burden I give you is light." (Matthew 11:30). This is super-duper news!!

I'm done with carrying needless, causeless, unnecessary burdens when Jesus said I don't have to. Jesus is the Word (John 1:1), His Word generated, initiated, and established everything in the universe, and His Word is the last and final Word. Therefore if Jesus said, "the burden I give you is light," then I should never be heavy.

I love being light, I love walking on air every day. I got this revelation on December of 2009, at a A/A meeting in the county jail. I was a chairperson for the meeting and it was like a light bulb went off in my mind, and a still small voice said, "Valerie, it you are trying to walk according to my will, you can not be weighed down by burdens, your flesh, and this world because my load is very light, and I have already overcome this world."

I couldn't believe what I was hearing God is so warm and tender, that He would take my anguished soul and make me light as a feather. How effective can I possibly be if I'm walking around overloaded with problems? I have been heavy I don't like it, I am light and I love it!!!! Walk in His bright light, and be light filled.

"The 21st of December"

On December 21st, 1998, God gave me more than I

Could ever dream of.

A Bright eyed baby girl full of love!!!

She defines beauty in every single way.

She is everything to me, her name is

Desiree.

The day she was born I will always

Remember

I got my Christmas present on the 21st of December!!

Day Twenty-One

"By wisdom a house is built, by understanding it is established, and by knowledge it's chambers are filled with all precious and pleasant riches"
(Proverbs 24:3,4)

To respect and be awe-struck by the Lord is wisdom, He leaves me speechless and that is very hard to do! He is so lovely, enchanting, and exquisite that it astounds me I love everything about Him.

The Bible says that our body is the temple of the Holy-Spirit(I Corinthians 6:19), and that is the house I am referring to today. By wisdom a house is built. Jesus said, ,"A wise man builds his house upon a rock.

(Matthew 7:24) Jesus said, "When the rain descended and the floods came, and the winds blew, and beat upon that house yet, it fell not for it was founded upon a rock (Matthew 7:25)
I want a house that doesn't fall when the winds of life come crashing upon it. I want a house that is still standing when a storm comes like a whirlwind. How do I achieve such a house? By wisdom, that's how!! Who but our God is a solid Rock?!! (Psalms18:31). I want to be absorbed, and consumed with my Lord and Savior, instead of settling for what will rot and pass away. His will is perfect, His Word has been tried, He is a buckler to all those that trust in Him (Psalm 18:30). I want a magnificent house that He is perpetually upon.

By understanding it is established, to understand is too comprehend, get the picture of it, to grasp and identify it, and let it penetrate inside you until it registers. I am not pretending to understand God in all His fullness however, He actually is working in me, to help me want to do, and be able to do what pleases Him (Phillipians 2:13), and often I do not understand until I obey. It is crazy and bizarre when His Word tells me to do something that I don't quite understand, and when I obey I get complete understanding. It is confounding and astounding when God gives you understanding for God is the King of all the earth; sing praises with understanding (Psalms 47:7). When you start understanding there is nothing left but a song on your heart.

By knowledge its chambers are filled with all precious and pleasant riches. I am so rich!! I know the One who is faithful, eternal, Holy, unchangeable, unsearchable, wise, available, glorious, majestic, compassionate, sovereign, strong, all powerful and in control! I am so rich with everything precious and pleasant. Anything that really has value or worth I have it because I have Jesus, absolutely nothing is missing.

Casting Crowns wrote a song called, " To know you is to want to know you more." Paul said, " I count all things but loss for the Excellency of the knowledge of Christ Jesus my Lord" (Philippians 3:8). It is by Knowledge(knowing), than we are filled with all pleasant and precious riches, Jesus said, " On judgement day many will say to me Lord, Lord, we prophesied in your name and cast out demons in your name and performed many miracles in your name. But I will reply I never knew you." (Matthew 7:22,23)

If you want your house to be full, adequate, plentiful, entire, stocked, and glorious then you need to know Jesus. Intimacy is Knowledge; knowing one another, ending each others sentences, laughing together, crying together, struggling together, triumphing together!!! I believe if you build your house(body) on wisdom, understanding, and knowledge, the material house that you live in will have all precious and pleasant riches!!!

To my very first grand-daughter
Olivia Grace Green
"Olivia Grace Green"

God has blessed this earth in an unusual way

He sent a baby girl from Heaven on St. Patricks Day.

She outdoes any shamrock by far

She is her mom and dad's lucky star!!

John and Brianne your eyes have witnessed something

more spectacular then they have ever seen!!!

God gave you a gift and her name is Olivia Grace

Green!!!

Day Twenty-Two

" If thou has thought evil lay thine hand upon thy mouth"
(Proverbs 30:32)

There is power of life and death in the tongue (Proverbs 18:21). God spoke and things started happening. God said "Let there be light" (Genesis 1:3), God said, "Let there be a space between the waters" (Genesis 1:6), God called the space sky, God calls those things that are not as though they are (Romans 4:17). In other words, He creates new things out of nothing with His mouth. However, before He starts speaking He thinks! I am challenging you today to choose your words carefully and prayerfully.

In November of 2009, God gave me this challenge, and it has turned my world upside down and inside out! I have what I say I have. I don't care if it is raining, snowing, and the earth is shaking, I have peace. I don't care if I am sneezing, coughing, and my nose is running: I am in excellent health, and by Jesus' stripes I am healed.

I don't care if my circumstances look bleak and hopeless, I have the hope of glory living inside of me and joy unspeakable. You may think I am delusional and not facing reality, however, I took God's challenge and decided to speak only Life out of my mouth, and I saw right before my own eyes His Word of Truth changing what looked beyond repair into something irreplaceable!!

How precious are God's thoughts unto us (Psalms 139:17) God's thought's toward us are precious. If we could just grasp the power of our thought life would guard our thoughts more closely. Our thoughts lead to our words. The Bible says," the fool utters all his mind" (Proverbs 29:11).

I don't want to hurt anybody no more with my words. I don't want to live a life of regrets because of what I said. I don't want to hurt people just because I am hurting. I can lay my hand upon my mouth when thoughts of evil cross my mind, and I can consider Jesus Christ and other people as the special, important, valuable beings that they are. Is it really satisfying, gratifying, and relieving when you yell at someone and say unkind words?

Is it really rewarding to put someone else down? I've had enough of damaging others with my thoughtless, careless, painful words. I refuse to do the devils dirty work. I am going to lift up, build up, and cheer up everyone I come in contact with. Today, if thou has thought evil lay thine hand upon thy mouth.

"Winter in the warmth of God's love"

He's the air that I breathe, yet He takes my Breath
away.
I feel Him in a snowflake, and beside me where I Lay.

In the anguish of winter He's my ray of Sun.

He quiets me with His love, the battle is already Won!

I see beyond my eyesight, I hear His sacred Word

I am taking care of the sparrow, your more valuable

than any Bird.

He diminishes my fears with His sweet, tender Voice

My whole being does back flips, He makes my soul

Rejoice

He's in the depths of my heart and in the Heavenliness

high Above

On a cold winter night I feel the warmth of Love.

Day Twenty-Three

" It is God's will for you to be content"
For I have learned in whatsoever state I am in there
with to be content (Philippians 4:13)

Wouldn't it be very nice today if you wanted nothing
more? Wouldn't it be pure delight to be tickled pink,
completely satisfied, and at ease? What if I told you
that this is God's will for you? Why else would God
say, " Be still and know that I am God"?

This same omnipotent God says that He will supply all
our needs according to His Glorious riches!! When are
we going to take God at His Word? "things" do not last
or fill you up! Things get old, things break down. Sure,
I've seen the commercials for that car that is built to
last, and then the next thing you know there is a recall
on that car. I seen beer commercials that promised a
good time, then I read the paper about a baby that was
killed by a drunk driver. All these things that promise
comfort and contentment are counterfeits.

People, things, and food will not fill that spot, and your heart will still be leaking and empty. I am telling you that I am sitting in a prison cell right, now, with a pair of department of corrections state browns on. Big house productions under-wear, and I am so comfortable in my own skin, and undisturbed by this world because I have learned that Jesus means business when he said, I am the resurrection and the life." (John 8:12) "and those who drink the water I give will never be thirsty again" (John 4:14).

You see contentment is not a fruit of the spirit, you don't automatically get it because you are born again. It is something learned out of close, substantial, inseparable, devoted and cozy relationship with Jesus Christ, when you draw close like this with Jesus everything else loses it's importance. Jesus gives your life total meaning, and serenity. Everything starts to make sense even if nothing makes sense!!!! Contentment is relaxing in the knowledge that God is sovereign and God is in control;. Only time that I am not content is when I am trying to fix events and control people, and the universe. God doesn't have to consult with me before he makes a flower sprout. He doesn't check in with me when it is time to send summer.

I am content because God got my back, because God is in control, because God will never leave me or fail me. Learn to be content by drawing near to God and I guarantee you'll be so satisfied you won't want anything more.

"Radical risk-taking faith"

Ark's get built and lives get saved,
When we step out in radical risk-taking faith.

Over 5,000 were full and were fed,
When a child of faith took a risk with his fish and his
bread.

They lowered his bed through a hole in a roof.

He walked away whole, faith always shows proof!

She was a virgin, only thing she knew about sex was
what she had heard.

It takes radical faith to say, "be it unto me according to
thy word."

Moses would rather suffer affliction than to enjoy the
pleasure of sin.

When God is on your side, you can't lose you can only
win!

Shadrach, Meshach, and Abednego would not bow, so
they did not burn.

Radical risk-taking faith can not be taught just learned.

It takes faith to believe he hears when you call

It is by, my God that I have leaped over a wall!!!

I'm not talking about getting your toes wet at the edge
of the ocean type of faith

I'm talking about sprinting forward, diving head first
in His ocean of grace.

It takes faith to live as a foreigner on this earth.

To love and cherish the one who orchestrated your
birth

It takes radical risk-taking faith to believe the invisible.

Jesus really moves mountains, he does the
impossible!!!!

Day Twenty Four

"It is too late when we die"

Did someone ever die that you knew, and you wished you would of said more, done more, cared more and loved more? Well it's too late when someone is dead!!!!

Jesus said, "I am the way, the truth, and the life, no man cometh to the Father except by Me." (John 14:6)

Today let's let Gods word speak directly to our hearts. "If thou for bear to deliver them that are ready to be slain; If thou sayest, behold we knew it not, doth not he that pondereth the heart consider it? And he that keepeth they soul doeth he know it? And shall not he render to every man according to his works?" (Proverbs 24:11,12) How beautiful are the feet that preach the gospel of peace and bring glad tidings of good things!!

How then shall they call on him in whom they have not believed? And how shall they hear without a preacher? So then faith cometh by hearing and hearing by the word of God (Romans 10:15,14,17).

If your are a born-again believer in Jesus Christ and have passed from death unto life and have been saved from the fiery depths of hell you have a duty to save others with fear pulling them out of the fire (Jude 23).

I just can't keep Christ to myself because I don't want anyone to go to hell, and be tormented for eternity. People are precious!! We just can not assume there is a trillion more moments! Things come unexpected such as; planes through buildings, drunk drivers, earthquakes, and much more God's word says, "When I say unto the wicked, thou shalt surely die; and thou givest him not warning, nor speakest to warn him from his wicked way, to save his life; the same wicked man shall die in his iniquity, but his blood will I require at thy hand. (EZ 3:18)

God is too good to keep to yourself, share him with those who don't know about his own dear Son. I don't want the devil to have one more, but its too late when they die.

"Finish Well"

When the pain that you're under seems too hard to

bear

And the hand you've been dealt seems completely

unfair

Keep pressing forward, God is already there!

Your running this race, you've stumbled, you've fell.

You've risen again, finish this race well!!!!

Day Twenty-Five

"When you are in yesterday or tomorrow, you are outside of God's will."
"This is the day that the lord has made let us rejoice and be glad in it" (Psalms 118:24)

Today we are going to stay in today! We are going to love, live, and laugh!!

Have you ever felt like you had more than you can handle? I will bet any amount of money that it is because of some fear of the future or some past regrets. God says, "as thy days so shall thy strength be." (Deut. 33:25) You only have enough strength for this very day. God is in this with you. He is your partner. I'm quite sure he is not frazzled and dazzled about this day. He not confused or shook. He is in complete control. God says forget the former things, do not dwell on the past. See, I am doing a new thing(Is 43:18).This day is new and so are you! The doors of yesterday are closed forevermore. You can't go backwards, God is right here, right now, longing to pour himself into you and rub himself all over. Jesus said, " and this is life eternal, that they might know thee the only true God, and Jesus Christ whom thou has sent." (John 17:13) to live life today is to know Jesus Christ, this should energize you to want to take this day on. We are not cowards; this day can not overcome us.

Jesus said nothing can separate us from him; not death nor life, neither angels nor demons, neither our fears for today nor our worries about tomorrow, not even the powers of hell can separate us from the love of God that is revealed in Christ Jesus our lord (Romans 8:38,39) Tomorrow can worry about itself, because I refuse to worry about it. This day, this moment is to precious to miss out on. I am not going to be consumed and absorbed with matters that are too great for me to figure out. God had already planned on giving me the abundant life before the foundation of the world and I plan on enjoying it today! Today is a victorious day! We will never see tomorrow because tomorrow will be today. If your are in yesterday or tomorrow you are outside of God's perfect will. His will is the very best, if you want the best stay in today.

To Butch and Mary Therese

Two towers of strength, two people calm in the midst

of the raging sea.

Two of the most loving people I have ever met that's

what you are to me.

Your spirits generate energy, love and peace.

I love you with everything inside me Butch and Mary

Therese.

You have been there countless times, all I had to do was

call

I have been blessed with the world's best mother and

father in law.

"Thank you Pastor Savage"

It happens every Tuesday in the chapel, we are gathered together in one place.

There is no condemnation, no petty arguments, There is only love and grace.

We are all on one accord desperately seeking God's face.

It is woman, sisters, friends, mom's, and our pastor

We are learning to be meek, and be controlled by our master.

To be anxious for nothing, prayer will get us places faster.

We laugh, we cry, and share our experiences as a mom.

In the midst of our storm there is an oasis of calm.

Words are inadequate to describe mom's in touch.

I'll try to keep it simple, and just say we need it very much.

In the chapel every Tuesday with God's blessing we are lavished.

We are so grateful that you invest your time into us,

Thank you Pastor Savage.

Day Twenty-Six

"Prayer is a rich rewarding experience"

Devote yourself to prayer; being watchful and thankful (Colossians 4:2) Pray without ceasing (1Thesalonians 5:17)

Wow! Wow! Wow! Where do I begin? Talking to God about anything and everything, anytime and anywhere, listening to His voice of love and Holiness whispering in my ears softly. I'm so in love with the lover of my soul. No one is going to die for me, He did!!! I have a solid, unbroken relationship with Jesus and it all happens through prayer. Now, wouldn't you say that prayer is a rich, rewarding experience? He knows my virtue, my faults, my weakness and my strengths and yet He never changes on me.

I never found anyone who spent every second of every day with me that didn't get sick of me but He can't get enough of me. I have never felt so loved, cherished and rich, He gives me the butterflies. He is explosive like dynamite. I can be totally naked and unashamed with my Lord, Savior, and Redeemer, and not feel one bit embarrassed. I don't have to say just the right thing or do something spectacular. I can just be myself and know beyond a shadow of a doubt that I am loved. I deeply desire that today you could experience God in the same way that I have.

It is an active, aggressive quest. It is prayer, it is communication; talking, listening, seeking, and finding what your heart has craved for your entire life. Your voice is so important to God. He probably tells Heaven to hush when you speak. If you been looking for someone who listens carefully and intently, who cares about every single detail of your life, who accepts the dirty, raunchy side as wel as the vibrant, dynamic, exceptional side, and who loves you from the top of your head to the souls of your feet, from the inside out then look no further!!!

God, Jesus, and the Sweet Holy Spirit want to love, comfort, help, counsel, guide, protect, give, and live every second of your life with you. Converse with God today and turn your carnival into an amusement park, turn your puddle into an ocean, turn your seed into an exotic flower, and turn your shallow life into an abundant life!!!! How? Through prayer!!!

Prayer really does change things! It is instant access to abundance. Soon as I open my eyes I demonstrate respect for life by humbly bowing on my knees and thanking God for a brand spanking new day. I say" good morning Daddy, good morning Jesus, good morning Sweet Holy Spirit," then I kiss them, and that may seem silly to you yet, it is one of the best moments of my day.

I pray all day, I love it! I really don't know your story, God may feel distant to you, you may be angry with God, and you may be waiting on God to answer your prayers. I don't pretend to understand it all. I do know that God is not inactive! Just because I haven't received the answer immediately, does not mean God is inactive. He may say "no Valerie," and guess what? That "no" may be the best play of my life. When you talk to God, there is this inner knowing that all is well because God does all things well, and you just know that you know that you are going to be alright and today I pray that you pray and find the richest experience of your life!!!!!!!

"A light in my tunnel"

Our trials in life are often misunderstood

God is able to turn what is bad into something good!!

Most people look for the light at the end of the tunnel

for hope,

It has been the in the tunnel that has helped me cope.

This light is so bright that darkness would run.

This light is the life it is God's only son!!!!!

Day Twenty-Seven

"Is God's will the miraculous?"

God is in the business of miracles, and I have a front row seat! I got saved in 1994, and I did not have one toe nail on my toes because I was frost bitten from living homeless on the streets of Philadelphia. I was on crack, alcohol, pills, and anything else I could get my hands on. I lived a life of crime, needless to say, I got arrested, and I went to a church service, and the woman leading the service said, "you can have all the drugs, crime, money, sex, and men you want, it will never satisfy, but Jesus says, "draw from my well it will never run dry." Tears started running down my cheeks like a fountain, and I ran to the front and asked, "How do I get to know Jesus?" She said, "seek him with all your heart", and she handed me a bible, well I read it day in and day out, and I can't explain it adequately in words but my life was transformed and I started to excel in everything.

First I got my G.E.D., then the prison sent me to Penn state college for physics, and political science, I received a 3.67 GPA in physics and a 4.0 GPA in political science. I graduated from manual accounting in 1995 and in 1996 I went on to bible college!! In December of 1996 I was paroled to a center and I continued in Bible College and found a church full of the Holy Spirit and love. God was there!!! Well this church was located in a bad area in Philadelphia, and they did outreaches, and fed the hungry, clothed the homeless, and loved everyone who entered. This is where I belonged, eventually I became a teacher there for ages nine to eleven years old. However, on the weekends I would take my oldest son and nephews and my newborn baby to an arcade in a nice area of Philadelphia, one Saturday in particular I lost my pocketbook at this arcade, and I had $156 in it and my WIC checks for my newborn daughter, so when I realized I lost my pocket-book, when I got home I got right on my knees and said, "Jesus you said if I have faith as much as a mustard seed I can tell a mountain to be cast in the sea and be removed, Jesus said if I ask that I will receive, so I am asking for my pocket book to be found in your name." Then I called my ex-husband and I told him what happened and he said, "Val chalk it up for a loss" and I said, "No! Jesus said if I ask I will receive." Well, he called me a Jesus freak and hung up on me. Then I went back to that arcade and told the owner I lost my pocketbook there, and he said, "One in a million chance you'll get that back." and I said, "Oh yes I will in Jesus' name." He told me to get out of his store and called me a loony toon.

Well the next morning was a Sunday and I told my pastor what happened and he said, "Valerie we will help you with formula for your daughter." and I said "thank you", and I am also believing Jesus for a miracle because nothing is too hard for him." So I stayed for the service, then I returned for the evening service, and when I walked in, the pastor asked me to come to the front of the church. Miraculously some one from my church (in the ghetto) was riding on the boulevard and thought they ran a cat over, and it was my pocket-book with everything in it!!!! Jesus is in the business of miracles!!! God is the arranger of things! Have faith in God, Jesus answered, "I tell you the truth, if anyone says to this mountain go throw yourself into the sea and does not doubt in his heart but believes that what he says will happen it will be done for him. Therefore I tell you, whatever you ask for in prayer, believe that you have received it, and it will be yours." (Mark 11:22-24) Jesus is the same yesterday, today, and forever.

He healed the sick, the lame, the blind, the deaf, and he said, "I tell you the truth anyone who believes in me will do the same works I have done and even greater works, because I am going to be with the father."(John 14:12) The first disciples took Jesus at His word, one day Peter and John were headed to the temple and they seen a man I am from birth, and they decided to use the name of Jesus Christ of Nazareth to heal and strengthen the lame mans legs, and it worked!!!(Acts 3:1-11) Jesus had already been killed and rose again when Peter and John performed this miracle, what does that tell you? Of course God's will is the Miraculous. If you really think about it every thing around us, and inside of us is truly miraculous. One night I just wanted something sweet but I didn't have anything, however, my room-mate was loaded with sweet stuff like dunking sticks, Swiss rolls, and a lot of chocolate but I didn't have the guts to ask her for any. So when I got in the bed the Sweet Holy-Spirit told me to ask her because she would say yes, but I said, "that's okay Jesus, I'll just wait for breakfast." Then I went to sleep. Well the next morning at 6:45am I was headed to breakfast and a friend of mine told me she had two Hershey bars for me, and I said, "Wow! Thank you!" and I was so grateful as a matter of fact I opened one on the spot and started eating it. So when I got back to my cell I started crying and thanking God for caring about every detail of my life. Well, that same day when I went to dinner, another woman walked up to me in the chow line and handed me a dunking stick. I was stupefied and so grateful and I said thank you so much. I thanked my daddy in heaven with all my heart because I know he is the father of every good and perfect gift.

So the very next day, I went to yard out at 1:30pm and I was walking around the track when another friend of mine pops her bible open and there is a Hershey bar right smack in the center of the bible! She told me that when she was running out of her cell for yard out that God told her to bring me a Hershey bar, she also told me that she usually don't part with her chocolate. I was totally blown away, and marveled at my king, master, and lover of my soul. Yet, if that just wasn't enough for me, later on that night I was in the common room playing cards when a young lady came waking up to the table I was at and handed me a Hershey bar!!! I know that I know that God's will is the Miraculous!

When you can see the invisible, you will see the impossible!! Please don't take my word for it, and think to yourself that maybe only certain people witness these miracles. Take God's written Word and see them for yourself. I experience the miraculous daily, and I want you to experience too.

For the past four nights the lord has been waking me up to pray for my sister Mickey, and this past week I have received four letters from her and she told me that my Mom has dementia.

Well this morning on April, 19, 2011 when I got on my knees I didn't know what to pray for my sister or my mom because my heart was torn in half, so I said, "Holy-Spirit, utter groans to the Father for me because I don't know how to pray today, and Jesus please intercede for my sister and my mom."

So I decided to get on my knees and just sing to the lord and let the Holy-Spirit and Jesus pray as I sang songs of praise, adoration, and victory. Well, when I went to do my daily devotion reading in the "upper room" for the April 19, 2011 It said, "the Spirit helps" and the scripture at the top of the page said, "we do not know how to pray as we ought but the Holy-Spirit intercedes with sighs too deep for words."(Romans 8:26) I started crying in amazement and gratitude, and the very first sentence read, "My elderly mother suffers from dementia", this is no coincidence. This is a living and real God who is intimate and miraculous. Yes! Yes! Yes! God's will is the miraculous.

"Daddy's little girl"

In 2009 I made a deliberate quality choice.
That I am a sheep, that needs to heed my shepherds
voice.

It's a long steady obedience in the same direction.
Letting patience have her perfect work that leads to
perfection.

Abiding, and remaining with Jesus in a very definite
way.
Overshadowed with His power every second of the
day.

When the enemy tried to influence my feelings with his
lies and deceit.
I lined my feelings up with truth and positioned him
under my feet.

My citizenship is in heaven, the kingdom is inside me.
I won't settle for what rot's, I have a specific word that
guides me!

His word runneth swiftly, it is powerfully alive!
When my flesh and my heart fail, God's strength is
where I thrive.

He whispers in my ears, "these trials are your companions,
They are not your foes.
He solves my problem's in advance, even when I don't know.

So I'm gliding through these difficulties supported totally by my king.
I have an oasis of calmness trusting Jesus with everything.

The comfort I receive from my comforter, is greater than my pain.
I don't know if there is room in my heart for the joy that I contain.

I walk awe-struck by my God all day long!!
Day after day I have within my heart a brand new song.

Living in His world is just so much brighter.
Casting all my cares upon Him has made my load lighter

In His presence I am undisturbed by this world
He is my daddy, and I'm his little girl.

Day Twenty-Eight

"God has raised us up together and made us sit together in heavenly places in Christ Jesus (Eph 2:6) Undisturbed by this world!"

Today is the day where your feet will be on earth but your heart will be up in heaven!!! When Jesus was raised from death, all those that believed on Him have been given an inheritance, and have been raised up together to sit in heavenly places with Him.

What in the world is she talking about, you may be thinking? I'm talking about not settling for the earth when you can be totally undisturbed by this world. I mean making a clean break from this world, and enjoy God's majesty all day, every day. Leave the humane and connect with the divine. See the invisible everywhere you look. We can be filled to the measure of all the fullness of God though faith (Ephesians 3:17-19).

The only way to experience this togetherness in the heavenliness with God is to believe that he wants you there with him, and that He is in complete control. To believe that nothing can happen to you without first passing through his mighty hands.

When you sit with Him in the heavenlies, he satisfies you more than the richest feast, even after this world has left you starving to death. I was starving for attention, I was starving for love, I was starving for joy and peace and there was no evidence of life inside of me, besides the fact that my heart was beating.

God has taken my body of death and unsettled emotions, and raised me up together with him in the heavens. I'm humbled, grateful and never coming back to this world. Experience God today. Stop looking inward, and start looking upward.

The psalmist said, "I will lift mine eyes unto the hills from whence cometh my help, my help cometh from the Lord, which made heaven and earth (Psalm 121:1,2) Today, I played a game of softball, and before I left my cell to go play, I asked Jesus to be my coach and I invited him to come play with me and he did!!

I had an awesome time, I had a ball! At one point I hit a foul, and I dropped the bat and went and grabbed my foul ball to help the other team and every body laughed and the activities instructor said, "Todd, what are you batting and catching?" and I said, " I just want to be helpful sir. "We won 4-3, and even if we didn't win it wouldn't matter to me because I can't lose because a winning spirit lives deep inside of me.

During the whole game I was caught up together with Christ in the heavens, it is the reason I dropped my bat and ran after the ball for the other team. I am servant of the most high God, and it is second nature for me to love and serve. I got the life! Jesus is life. Sit with him today in the heavens, undisturbed by this world.

"Perfect Fit"

I feel so cherished and loved by you.

Jesus you are too good to be true!

I want to give you all I can.

You love me just for who I am.

In my heart the counterfeits of love have died.

Your endless, measureless love keeps me electrified.

Words are besides the point, and truly inadequate.

Your outside of space and time, yet in my heart you're

the perfect fit.

Day Twenty-Nine

"Locked and loaded on God's Will"

Today we are going to get entangled, absorbed, consumed, engrossed, and totally locked and loaded on God's will.

This is not about you, this is about God!!! When you are locked into something, it is secure and immovable. I am challenging you get locked into God! This is a place that you can not be shook or moved. To be loaded with something, is to be full of something. Today be full of God!

An unloaded gun will not do any damage. It would be foolish for a hunter to go hunting with an unloaded rifle. In the same way it is very foolish to start your day without God. Without God life is missing, peace is missing, and love is missing.

I don't know about you but I want to be secure and full. I've been insecure and empty and I hated it. I was full of myself, yet containing nothing. I had no substance, now I am solidly built because I emptied myself out, and got locked and loaded on God.

When your locked and loaded with God your mind, speech, and actions are firmly established in Him, and believe me when I tell you that you will not miss out on a single blessing. Plug yourself into power. Join yourself to Jesus. A fan unplugged is useless. A car without a motor will not run. You, without Jesus are lifeless!!!! Get locked and loaded on life right this second by inviting Jesus to be inside you and beside you through out this whole day, and every day!! My true freedom is being locked and loaded up with Jesus!!!!

At 5:47 AM on May thirtieth, 2012 my Sweet Holy Spirit planted this in my heart." The journey is the reward"

This journey has been your reward with the pain,

exposure, disclosure, and of course all the fun!!!!

Valerie, look back only to remember the victory's you

have won.

You were called to finish this race, not just start it.

When you get to your red seas they will be departed.

You have done what is necessary to begin a new life.

Celebrate every moment of it with Jesus Christ.

At 11:30 AM I got my release date.

Day Thirty

"Inviting and exciting"

I am bursting with excitement because what no one ever thought could happen is the very thing God prepared for those who love Him!!! (1Corinthians 2:9)

Do you want a life full of color and spice? Do you want something that lasts? Do you want to rise again? Jesus is the resurrection and life!!! (John 11:25) Jesus is the way, the truth, and the life. (John 14:6) Invite Him into your heart, and ask Him to explode inside of you. Get covered, get hidden, get buried in Jesus' love. Get satisfied by his endless love.

I am going to exalt and magnify my lord today. I am so sick and tired of magnifying my problems, my fears, my issues, my pain, my guilt, and under sizing my God! I'm taking God out of the box I kept Him in, and giving Him His rightful place in my life! It is down right useless to fight against God's will, and why would I anyway when it is soooooooooo inviting and exciting? Why would I waste my day when I can spend time with Jesus?!!

You just don't experience life the same way any more after you started sharing every moment with Jesus. You start seeing everything and everyone differently. You look at the sky so different when you intimately know the one who designed it and hand crafted it with his own hands. You don't just walk by needy people any longer without caring. You start making a donation and contribution to life instead of sucking everything and everyone dry! You launch into the rocket of God's boundless inviting, exciting will with no regrets and no question. You don't sleep with one eye open anymore or keep looking over your shoulder because there is no law against what the holy-spirit produces. There is only freedom, peace, joy, kindness, patience, faithfulness, gentleness, and self-control. (Galatians 5:22'23)

It is obvious that there are consequences for every choice we make, especially since I write this from a prison cell and I am not trying to give anyone a false notion that serving God is like tip-toeing through the tulips. However, in the midst of painful circumstances I have found an anchor for my soul and He is a person that has united Himself to me, and our amazing oneness has given me a security that I have never known.

I am head over heels in love with Jesus!! I love His love! Yesterday I slow danced with Him three times. I had an indescribable, unnatural, joy unspeakable feeling that I just can't fully express. He is my valentine all year round. I was in the middle of exercising, and a song came on and tears started coming down my eyes and I said, "Jesus, I stand in awe of you, and I just am going to slow dance with you right now," and I did!! One song after the other I sang to Him and slow danced with Him. It was special.

I didn't feel one bit embarrassed because I know I have His approval, acceptance, and love!! To know where you stand with God is exhilarating! I stand gloriously complete!! I am whole!! He has made me believe that I was worth dying for.

I lived with the belief for years that I wasn't worth a nickel yet, the Sweet Holy Spirit whispered in my ears, "your priceless to me." this is a no brainier, God's will is inviting and exciting.

Today invite the Father, Jesus, and the Sweet Holy Spirit into your heart, soul, and mind. Now I am not saying that your circumstances will change but I am saying that you will change by a God who never changes. every day you know His love is the same, His compassions are new, His forgiveness is deeper than the sea, His tender mercies are over all His works, His sovereignty is on display, His holiness is astounding, and His strength is immovable and unshakeable!! Just talking about His character and nature excites me.

I invite you to God's exciting will today, and I sincerely pray from the depths of my heart that you receive this invitation gladly. God's will is so wonderful it is exciting to obey. I awake in expectation, longing for what will be next.

"In closing"

There it is, it is finished!!!!!! Get on your knees right now, and invite Him into the throne of your heart to reign forevermore in every area of your life. Confess with your mouth that Jesus is Lord and believe whole heartedly that he died for your sins, and three days later he rose and conquered death.

He will also raise your life to unexplainable heights, and you will receive unimaginable blessings. Go back to day one and start your adventure all over again with excitement and of course with Jesus receive your vast inheritance because He is your exceeding great reward. This is a deliberate choice and commitment of newness of life, only the fool says in his heart there is no God!!!! (Psalm 14:1)

Made in the USA
San Bernardino, CA
26 July 2018